D0708065

Columbia University

Contributions to Education

Teachers College Series

No. 486

AMS PRESS
NEW YORK

AN EVALUATION OF GUIDED STUDY AND SMALL-GROUP DISCUSSION IN A NORMAL SCHOOL

156741

By

GERTRUDE TYSON SHIPLEY, Ph.D.

TEACHERS COLLEGE, COLUMBIA UNIVERSITY
CONTRIBUTIONS TO EDUCATION, No. 486

LB1731
S5
1972

BUREAU OF PUBLICATIONS
Teachers College, Columbia University
NEW YORK CITY
1932

Library of Congress Cataloging in Publication Data

Shipley, Gertrude Tyson, 1888-
    An evaluation of guided study and small-group dis-
cussion in a normal school.

    Reprint of the 1932 ed., issued in series: Teachers
College, Columbia University. Contributions to education, no. 486.
    Originally presented as the author's thesis, Columbia.
    Bibliography: **p.**
    1. Teachers, Training of. 2. Study, Method of.
3. Education--Study and teaching. I. Title. II.
Series: Columbia University. Teachers College. Contributions to education, no. 486.
LB1731.S5 1972   378.1'7   73-- 177787

    ISBN 0-404-55486-5

Reprinted by Special Arrangement with Teachers
College Press, New York, New York

From the edition of 1932, New York
First AMS edition published in 1972
Manufactured in the United States

AMS PRESS, INC.
NEW YORK, N. Y.   10003

ACKNOWLEDGMENTS

I am glad to have this opportunity to express my indebtedness to those who have helped with this study.

I wish first to express my appreciation to the members of my dissertation committee—Dr. J. R. McGaughy (chairman), Dr. Edward S. Evenden, and Dr. Robert B. Raup—for their continued guidance, help, and encouragement.

I thank Mr. Frederick Holtz, principal of Maxwell Training School for Teachers, for permission to carry on the experiment, and Dr. William J. Taylor, head of the Department of Psychology and Education at the same institution, for the privilege of being allowed to teach only one subject for an entire school year and for his coöperation throughout the study.

My appreciation is extended also to those who contributed by judging the anonymous statements of the students.

G. T. S.

CONTENTS

TABLES

CHAPTER I

THE PROBLEM

Examination of current literature leads the writer to agree with Dr. Bagley [1] that the "quantitative movement in higher education seems to be a fairly virgin field." This is especially true regarding controlled experimentation in the field of methods or classroom teaching procedure. Naturally one puzzles over such statements as that of Gentry,[1] "Quantitative measurement on the college level is now about where it was a decade ago in high school or where elementary schools were twenty years ago." Is Dr. Kilpatrick [1] right in saying that quantitative measurement in higher education has contributed little and that so far it has done as much harm as good? Is controlled experimentation on the college level not feasible, not worth while, or are there other reasons which may account for the apparent paucity of scientific studies? [2]

Especially noticeable is the dearth of reliable data concerning methods of instruction on this level. This seems unusual in view of the fact that so much has been said, written, and published on methods of teaching in the elementary and in the high school fields. Many carefully controlled experiments, e.g., Coryell's.[3] have proved conclusively that methods of teaching do influence results achieved by pupils on both these levels and that that influence may be readily perceived.[4]

Another question arises. Has teaching on levels above the high school an entity so much its own and a purpose so distinct that none of the procedures found to be of value on the lower levels are applicable to it in any sense, or even worthy of analysis?

[1] Quoted in the *Eighteenth Yearbook* of the National Society of College Teachers of Education. pp. 179–89, 1930.
[2] Judd, C. H., "The School of Education." *Higher Education in America* (edited by R. A. Kent), pp. 157–92, 1930.
[3] Coryell, Nancy Gillmore, *An Evaluation of Extensive and Intensive Teaching of Literature.* Contributions to Education, No. 275. Bureau of Publications, Teachers College, Columbia University, 1927.
[4] This study will be confined to the college level.

1

Investigation of available published material tends to show that a variety of circumstances has contributed to the present status of methods of teaching on the college level.

With the exception of a few studies, to be analyzed later, the public has had to rely in the main on the subjective judgments of educational leaders, and on the results of questionnaires sent to those in the field, for evidence as to which methods of teaching are used in the college classroom and their relative values. This type of evidence is of great value, but even conscientious answering of questionnaires on this subject and the most careful tabulation of results leave doubts in the mind of the investigator in this field concerning the validity of the evidence. There frequently occur statements such as, "I am not sure," "I think," or "I have tried certain of the new methods and think they are good but have no proof of the results being better."

Another contributing circumstance is the conflict of opinion that exists concerning methods of teaching on the college level. Again and again, published statements are found to the effect that teaching on the college level is decidedly poorer than that on the lower levels,[5] that knowledge of subject-matter alone, vitally important as it is, does not insure efficient teaching,[6] that college instructors should be required to take methods courses before being allowed to teach their various subjects,[5] that no other educational unit is so completely tradition-bound as higher education.[7]

On the other hand, there are vigorous statements to the effect that a college or university teacher needs nothing more than a thorough knowledge of the subject matter to be taught, that "in a quantitative movement there is danger of losing the qualitative side,"[8] the possibility that emphasis upon measurement may adversely affect teaching, that a college teacher is a specialist and capable of working out his own methods, and that the subject-matter of college courses is too highly differentiated to permit even the smallest amount of standardization of methods of presentation.[9]

[5] *American Association of University Professors*, Vol. XVI, No. 5, University of Colorado.

[6] Zook, G. F., "Major Problems of Improvement of Instruction in Higher Institutions." *School and Society*, 30: 277–82, August 31, 1929.

[7] Kelly, F. J., Education Monographs, 1925–26. *Needed Research in Higher Education*.

[8] Foster, I. O., quoted by Manuel, Herschel T., in *Eighteenth Yearbook* of National Society of College Teachers of Education, pp. 179–80, 1930.

[9] Stokes, G., quoted by Manuel, Herschel T., in *Eighteenth Yearbook* of National Society of College Teachers of Education, p. 188, 1930.

BRIEF SURVEY OF RELATED STUDIES

The foregoing paragraphs are not intended to convey the idea that there has been absolutely no quantitative measurement movement on the college level, but that there has been comparatively little. There have been, as was mentioned before, a few carefully controlled experiments which have produced highly valuable evidence. The very nature of the experiments tends to show that there has been a growing and spreading belief that something must be done to reduce the high academic mortality,[10] to improve methods of teaching on the college level, to make them more lifelike and social, and that results obtained from the use of certain method procedures on secondary levels might tend to indicate that these methods possibly could be of value on the next higher level.

Examination of summaries of analyses already made of college teaching quantitatively measured [11] yields evidence that might be used for and against the employment of the "newer methods" on the upper levels.

These experiments have included, among others, quantitative measurement in such studies as problem versus lecture, lecture versus class discussion, lecture-recitation versus supervised individual instruction, the value of the quiz, of varying amounts of laboratory work, of more student activity, and the optimum size of a class.

Those studies that deal more directly with methods of classroom procedure have centered in the main around comparison of the traditional lecture method with various forms of socialized procedure and various types of study procedures.

Hudelson [12] (in his 873 [12a] separate experiments on class size) found that students of larger classes measured in terms of examination and class marks made a better showing than those in smaller classes. These experiments made no attempt to evaluate concomitant learnings.

[10] Pressey, L. C., in *Eighteenth Yearbook* of the National Society of College Teachers of Education, p. 177, 1930.

[11] Hudelson, Earl, "Survey of Investigations Using Quantitative Criteria in Education." *Eighteenth Yearbook* of the National Society of College Teachers of Education, 1930. And— Good, Carter V., "Methods of Teaching in Training School." *Journal of Higher Education*, 1: 391–95, October, 1930, 453–66, November, 1930.

[12] Hudelson, Earl, *Problems of College Education*, Chap. XXXII. University of Minnesota Press, 1928.

[12a] Hudelson, Earl, "Are Classes Too Large?" *Journal of Higher Education*, 1: 436–39, November, 1930.

Hurd and Lyon [13] found that learning in the sciences investigated was facilitated by increasing the amount of laboratory work.

Barnes found,[14] in his analysis to evaluate extra quiz sections, that the gain made through them was of no significant value and did not warrant extra time even when given extra credit

Tuttle,[15] in his comparison of the use of the project and lecture methods in giving a course in educational psychology, found a gain in favor of the project method when the students had had previous training in psychology, but found no significant difference when there had been no previous training.

Davis [16] found, in connection with teaching a course in elementary unified mathematics, that when he compared the lecture-recitation with the supervised-individual method in terms of mean scores on standardized tests, the latter method scored a gain over the former, but that final grades over two quarters favored the lecture-recitation method by 12 per cent. He felt that in reality there was no significant superiority either way.

Morris,[17] in his experiment at the University of Oregon to determine the relative effectiveness of the problem and lecture method in a course in principles of economics, found the following statements to be true: (1) For those students paired as to intelligence the problem-project method proved superior. (2) For those equated on basis of previous marks the lecture was even more significantly superior. (3) When both scores were thrown together the average mean score was practically identical under the two methods. This held for students of both high and low mentality.

Bane,[18] in his experiment with lecture versus class discussion, found that the two methods were equally effective in immediate recall of content-material; class discussion yielded better results for delayed recall; lecturing was more suitable for the immediate recall of subject matter than for its retention, while the reverse was true of class-discussion method.

Spence [19] found the lecture method superior in his graduate

[13] Hurd, A. W., *Problems of Science Teaching at the College Level.* University of Minnesota, 1929.

[14] Douglas, Harl, and Others: University of Oregon, Publication Vol. I, No. 7, Education Series, February, 1929.   [15] *Ibid.*   [16] *Ibid.*, 12.   [17] *Ibid.*

[18] Bane, C. L., "The Lecture vs. the Class-Discussion Method of College Teaching." *School and Society,* 21: 300–02, March 7, 1925.

[19] Spence, R. B., "Lecture and Class Discussion in Teaching Educational Psychology." *Journal of Educational Psychology,* 19: 454–62, October, 1928.

course in psychology in the outcomes measured by the tests he employed.

Greene,[20] in his comparison of lectures with individual reading as a method of teaching, found that for immediate results there were no differences except that brighter students tended to profit more by the experimental or reading method.   In delayed recall the lecture method proved superior.

Peters [21] performed an interesting parallel-group experiment in psychology, in which he tried out the study-conference versus the recitation plan of teaching.   He arranged an hour's reading period each week.   The students used a set of study questions and individually consulted the teacher, who was on hand during this period.   This group had also an hour's group discussion every two weeks.   The control group had one hour of recitation, and, supposedly, two hours of home study each week.   Results of objective intra-term tests and a final examination using the May Standardized Test on Woodworth's *Psychology* were the bases for judging results.   The experimental group excelled by approximately 10 per cent on six of the eight tests; on the other two tests the control group excelled by a like amount.   The latter two were on the topics of will and reasoning.   Chances against reversal of results were found to be 13.5 to 1.

In a comparison of two methods of study procedure in connection with the teaching of a course in educational psychology, Crow [22] found that in every case the groups having extra-class study gained more relatively than did the groups which confined study to class periods.   In the delayed recall tests, however, the classroom study groups retained more of what they had learned.   Two instructors, each teaching in a different state, participated in this study.   The students in one state had had a previous course in psychology while the other students had not.

Need for This Study

The evidence offered by the experiments here summarized, and by others more or less like them, shows a surprising lack of agree-

[20] Greene, E. B., *The Relative Effectiveness of Lectures and Individual Reading as Methods*, Genetic Psychology Monographs, 4: 459–63, December, 1928.

[21] Peters, C. C., Unpublished study at Pennsylvania State College.

[22] A Ph.D. study at New York University.   For a brief summary of this study, see Crow, L. D., "The Comparative Value of Extra-Classroom Study in the Learning of Educational Psychology." *Journal of Educational Research*, 22: 215–18, October, 1930.

ment, which may or may not be due to a difference in variables which could not be controlled.   Such factual and experimental evidence must be greatly enlarged if certain teaching techniques which have been proved of value on the elementary and high school levels are either to be accepted and used, or discarded. Investigations made tend to indicate that college instruction can be scientifically studied, not merely described, and that it can be experimentally, and, in some phases, quantitatively evaluated.

This small fund of evidence relative to effective teaching on the college level and personal teaching problems stimulated the writer to make this study.

STATEMENT OF PROBLEM

The immediate problem was that of how best to teach a course in principles of education to six groups of seniors in a four-year normal school (Maxwell Training School for Teachers, Brooklyn, New York).[23]   The writer considered the following: Should a course involving, among many other factors, a formulation of points of view be based upon a single text?   What method of procedure would drive the students outside the one text assigned to the course, would stimulate them to think for themselves, and to formulate their own points of view and analyze them critically, instead of blindly accepting those offered by their instructors? How could they be helped to gain in their ability to support points of view with authoritative information and, when challenged, to defend these same points of view within reason rather than to accept passively and approve that which an instructor had said?   How could they be encouraged to read more widely, yet more selectively and critically?   Might essential reading done to satisfy the requirements of this course, if carefully selected and guided by thought-provoking questions, stimulate students to further reading on their own account?   Might this reading aid in helping the individual to acquire the mature reading habit which means that he has the desire to read, reads when he does not have to, has wide or at least varied reading interests, and ponders over what he has read and is to read?   Could any of these factors be provided for without adding to already overloaded schedules?   Could they, by any possibility, be cared for

[23] In 1931, Maxwell Training School for Teachers became a four-year teacher-training college.

in such a way as not to increase, but rather appreciably to reduce, out-of-school study?

It will be recognized that the experimenter was forced to take cognizance of such problems as were described in the foregoing paragraphs. Experimentation, however, necessitated an analysis of the teaching situation from other angles which might influence the selection of the problem.

First of all these seniors were carrying twenty-four hours of recitation out of a twenty-five-hour school week, and the twenty-fifth hour was given to compulsory attendance upon the weekly school assembly. The subjects numbered twelve in all, including the subject matter called for in their gymnasium work. Reference material in the school library for the course in principles of education was inadequate, both in quantity and quality. A check-up showed that many of the students' homes were remote from public libraries, and that very few of the branch libraries were at all up-to-date in educational reference material. As has been said before, there seemed to be a reluctance on the part of the students to give personal opinions even about issues avowedly controversial, and a tendency, in spite of what an instructor might say, to accept as the one and final authority the text allotted to a course. Even though a book used might be out-of-date, they seemed to feel a final argument might be, "Well, the book says that."

Careful analysis of all factors influencing the situation, of how best to get experimental data and yet safeguard the students, and how to avoid what sometimes prove to be disastrous results of so-called experimental exploitation, led to the formulation of the following problem for experimentation:

Problem

Will the use of small group-study discussion periods during one or two hours of a three-hour a week course in principles of education reduce the required extra-class study appreciably, yield any concomitants of value, and yet enable the students concerned to achieve as good results, measured by objective tests, as if all three class periods had been given to class discussion and all the assigned reading had been done outside the class period?

CHAPTER II

THE EXPERIMENT

SETTING UP THE EXPERIMENT

Grouping

Thirteen classes of seniors (383 students[1] in all), taking a course in principles of education participated in the experiment, seven classes during the winter semester (September to February 1929–30) and six classes during the spring term (February 1930 to July 1930). With the exception of the handling of the objective data and the findings and interpretation of the statistical data, the two experiments will be discussed as one. This is possible since, with the exception of one factor, conditions were the same during both semesters. The wording of the objective test questions was not identical in both semesters, so the data will be computed and interpreted as if two separate experiments were being reported.[2]

The organization of the various class groups, an administrative one of numerical basis, could not be disturbed. These groups were equated on the multiple bases plan as follows:[3]

Bases Used [4]	Weight
1. Chronological Age (in months)...........................	2
2. Otis Intelligence Scores.................................	3
3. Practice Teaching Scores...............................	0.5
4. Personality Ratings.....................................	1
5. Freshman Averages (weighted by hours)..................	2

The various bases were selected as being those available measures which were most reliable as an index of abilities essential to coping with a course in principles of education. Constancy was the standard of weighting; therefore Otis intelligence scores received the heaviest weighting, chronological age and Freshman averages the next, and so on.

---

[1] Forty-two students' records had to be discarded because the students either were absent from one or more of the objective tests or because there were no intelligence test scores available.

[2] First experiment: four control and three experimental classes. Second experiment: three control and three experimental classes.

[3] McCall, William A., *How to Experiment in Education*, Chap. 3, pp. 29–31. Macmillan, 1923.

[4] Statistical treatment will be found in Chapter III of this study.

No initial test was given. No standardized test was available which would give a reliable index of ability to reason, to select and weigh facts, and to evaluate principles. As far as could be seen, a test set up by the experimenter of so broad and general a nature as the field, of necessity, would demand, would in all probability yield no more reliable indexes than those measures already used. The fact that the students participating in the experiment had had about the same elementary and high school education, had gained entrance to a three-year teacher-training school, and had taken about the same courses after entrance (electives coming only in the senior year), and the further fact that the failures had been weeded out during the two previous years might be viewed as further equating factors.

The selection of the groups to be exposed to the experimental procedure was made at random during the first week of the course in both semesters. The instructor did not know the students personally, which helped to make this selection even more of a random one.

The Teaching Procedure

Periods Common to Both Control and Experimental Groups

The course in principles of education met three fifty-minute periods a week. During the recitation periods the students and teacher participated in discussion on the various topics assigned to the subject. The discussion centered around questions grouped under topical headings which the instructor had incorporated in a syllabus.[5] Each topic was accompanied by paginated references. (See Appendix A for outline of the course.) These questions [6] served a twofold purpose. They were designed primarily to guide the students' reading and to guide, but not dominate, the discussion. During this experiment they served the added purpose of stabilizing the teaching procedure and of insuring all thirteen classes covering the same material and attacking the discussion from the same angle.[7]

Both the experimental and the control classes had the same

[5] A syllabus such as the one mentioned above is used by the writer in connection with all courses she gives, so it is not peculiar to the experimental situation.

[6] Many other questions were used by the instructor to stimulate divergent thinking or were asked by students seeking further information.

[7] This did not constitute the entire teaching procedure. Individual book and magazine reports, and class debates were also used, but even here whatever was given to one class was given to all thirteen.

type of so-called "recitation period." The control classes, however, had three of these general class-discussion periods a week, whereas the experimental classes had either one or two. Their other periods were given to small-group discussions and directed study. At times the class discussion of one of the questions mentioned above would occupy the entire recitation period. Frequently a student would ask a question of her own or offer an opinion. When these were referred to the members of the class for their reaction, vigorous argument often resulted. Illustrations were drawn from their own life situations. Activities of their school and class (student government, social affairs, faculty-student relationships, etc.) furnished material for these illustrations. Now and again a student, in her enthusiasm to prove or disprove a bit of theory or opinion, would offer a statement that could easily be traced to some personal home or social experience. At times the writer wondered whether or not it was wise to permit such intimate personal statements. The students, however, seemed entirely free of self-consciousness in their discussions. Since educational principles are supposed to help in personal, as well as classroom, adjustments, since out-of-school life is quite as valuable from the educational point of view as that within the school, nothing was done to curb absolute freedom of statement. There was one exception. When the students spoke of their various classroom experiences while engaged in practice teaching there was a tendency to mention schools by number and teachers by name. With guidance, however, they soon learned to avoid these particular personal factors.

At all times the instructor endeavored to be a member of the group, offering her opinions not arbitrarily, but merely as contributions having value because they were the outgrowth of a richer, fuller, and more mature experience. Rarely did she have to stimulate the discussion, but more often had to check its impetus. That same enthusiasm, spoken of before, and a seeming lack of previous opportunity for freedom in classroom discussion were instrumental in causing a remark to be made now and then to which a student of another nationality, race, church affiliation, or social sphere might take personal exception although this had been farthest from the intention of the pupil making the statement. It was also the instructor's responsibility to prevent the discussion's digressing too much, and to preserve a balance of treatment between the topics, although a course of such a general nature as one in principles of education should offer many opportunities for excursions into associated fields. Some students had to receive help in learning the value of backing up their own opinions with those of authorities in the field—when such material was available.

Directed Study and Group Discussion

The small-group periods were given to discussing the questions in the syllabus and studying or reading reference material within groups limited to five or six members. The students had made up their own groups, selected their own leaders, and were free to proceed as they thought best. The instructor was at hand ready and willing to give help if it was desired, but did not go to any group unless specifically requested to do so.[8] From ten to fifteen reference books were available for the students to use. Most of these were references listed in the syllabus, although from time to time these were augmented by current magazine and newspaper clippings pertinent to the topic under discussion.

These groups worked at their own rate of speed, the only requirement being that they keep their discussion well ahead of that of the class, in order that the latter should not be retarded because the students were unprepared.

Two of the experimental classes (single experimental) had one of these periods a week and two class-discussion periods (both semesters), whereas one experimental class (double experimental) each semester had two of these small-group discussion periods each week and only one class period. These latter groups did not study, throughout the experiment, outside these two periods.[9]

The writer refrained from sitting in on the discussions of the small groups for obvious reasons. It was necessary to keep constant the amount of help given the groups. In order to increase the students' sensitiveness to their own difficulties it·seemed de-

[8] This necessitated the instructor's being well versed in the material of the references if effective help were to be rendered these small groups, otherwise the group would lose time while waiting for her to look up context motivated by a question.

[9] No pledges were asked and "home work" was not forbidden. The only request made was that if the students found it necessary to do "home work" they make a statement of the fact. They stated after the final examination that they had done no extra-class studying.

sirable to cause them to seek help from the instructor on their own initiative.   Traditional disinclination to ask any help of a teacher gradually gave place to finer distinctions of what constitutes legitimate requests for help.   The instructor gave such help as was needed to give the discussion further impetus.

The experiment hinged, then, on the fact that the control classes did all their studying individually outside class periods, whereas the experimental classes had one or two small-group discussions and directed study periods a week.   Those classes having two small-group periods a week did all their studying in the one period assigned for that purpose, and those having one small-group period augmented that by home study of the assigned text (Thorndike and Gates *Elementary Principles of Education*) if they felt they needed to do so.

The Testing Procedure

All the students in the thirteen classes were given a series of objective tests at intervals during the semesters.

Since there were no reliable criteria known to the experimenter with which to compare these tests she had to rely upon her own judgment as to their validity.   This judgment, however, seemed to be substantiated by the results obtained in the final examination which was compiled and administered by the education department.   The questions were contributed by the instructors teaching the course and by the head of the department.

This departmental examination was comparable in type and content to the tests devised by the writer.   Both were objectively administered and scored.   Both included false and true statements, multiple choice, association, and completion questions. Precautions were taken in formulating the completion questions so that no variation in response was possible.

In both the term tests and the final examinations some questions checked the pupils' factual knowledge of the required subject matter, others, their ability to interpret practical situations in the light of theoretical principles already learned, while still others checked their ability to see the significance of historical educational trends in present educational procedures.

Statistical data to be presented in Tables 11 and 12 in Chapter III seem to be evidence that the experimental classes in the final examination were superior, as measured by this examination, to the control classes. That all members of both the control and the experimental classes had to meet the requirements of a final examination that included judgments other than those of the writer, is evidence in addition to the statistical data of the validity of the testing procedure.

Because of the ruling of the school that students must receive grades as soon as possible after taking an examination, the tests were graded each time. No statistical comparison of the data, however, was made until the close of the repetition of the experiment, as the writer wished to remain in ignorance of the relative standing of the various groups until the entire experiment had been completed.

CHAPTER III

STATISTICAL TREATMENT AND EVALUATION OF DATA

STATISTICAL CLASSIFICATION OF GROUPS

The groups participating in the experiment were classified on the bases of chronological age (in months), Otis scores,[1] practice teaching grades,[2] freshman averages,[3] and personality ratings.[4]

In order to compare the equation data of the various groups, and also the objective test evidence, the critical ratio technique of Dr. J. R. McGaughy[5] was applied to the various items. This technique is that of comparing two groups by averages or other central tendencies; with a careful measuring of the significance of the differences between the averages in any one item (e.g., Otis scores). This critical ratio measure makes it possible to state what the probability of chances is that an obtained difference will not vary beyond certain designated limits; in other words, were the measure repeated, the obtained difference would not yield a difference in favor of the other, or competing measure.

The raw data were distributed (guessed mean technique) and the various tendencies were computed by the following formulae.

Measure of Central Tendency:

$$\text{True Mean} = \text{Mid-point} + \frac{\Sigma \text{ frequency dev.}}{\text{No. of cases}} \times \text{step interval}$$

Measure of Variability:

$$\text{Standard Deviation (sigma)} = \sqrt{\frac{\Sigma f d^2}{\text{No.}} - \left(\frac{\Sigma f d^2}{\text{No.}}\right)} \times \text{step interval}$$

---

[1] Otis Self-Administering Tests of Mental Ability: Higher Examination (for high schools and colleges).

[2] These grades are given by critic teachers while the students are practice-teaching in the schools.

[3] This average is the mean of the term averages in each subject (weighted by hours), given by instructors in the theory department.

[4] This rating is a composite one based on mentality, industry, social attributes, appearance, speech, etc.

[5] McGaughy, J. R., *The Fiscal Administration of City School Systems*, Appendix B. Macmillan, 1924.

14

Measure of Reliability of Mean:

$$\text{Probable Error of Mean} = \tfrac{2}{3} \text{ of } \frac{\text{S.D.}}{\sqrt{\text{No.}}}$$

Measure of Reliability of Difference of Means:

$$\text{P.E. of Difference of Means} = \tfrac{2}{3} \sqrt{\frac{\sigma A^2}{\text{No.}_A} + \frac{\sigma B^2}{\text{No.}_B}}$$

Measure of Significance of the Difference between two Means:

$$\text{Critical Ratio} = \frac{M_1 - M_2}{\text{P.E.}_{\text{Diff. of Means}}}$$

The accepted standard for interpreting the size of the obtained difference is that when the critical ratio is 3.0 or more, the mean chances are less than 1 to 46 that the true difference can be as small as zero.

Table 1 gives the classification of groups for the first experiment, and Table 2 shows the significance of differences in classification data. Table 3 shows the classification of groups for the second experiment, and Table 4 the significance of differences in classification data for that experiment.

It is possible to discuss the classification data of both experiments at one and the same time because the same bases were used and the various tables in both showed marked similarities.

Examination of all sections of Table I yields the following facts. The classes are for all practical purposes homogeneous when group measures are considered. Even weighting seems to make very little difference.[5a]

First Experiment:	* SA^5	SA^7	SA^8	SA^9	SA^{10}	SA^{11}	SA^{12}
E. C. M. E. C..........	.47	.48	.51	.48	.49	.46	.48

Second Experiment:	SA^5	SA^6	SA^7	SA^8	SA^9	SA^{10}
E. C. M. E. C..........	.55	.52	.50	.44	.51	.49

* Senior A (first semester of senior year).

There is no formula for computing this probable error but it would in all likelihood be large, thus tending to show even more homogeneity. This can be concluded because the obtained differences between each possible pairing of groups, with one exception, were so small as to show a 1 to 21 chance or more that

[5a] McCall, *How to Experiment in Education*, p. 170. Experimental Coefficient of the Mean

$$\text{Experimental Coefficient} = \frac{\text{M E C}}{2.78 \text{ S D M E C}}$$

TABLE 1

CLASSIFICATION OF GROUPS BY AVERAGES ON BASIS OF OTIS SCORES,
CHRONOLOGICAL AGE, PRACTICE GRADES, PERSONALITY
TRAITS, AND FRESHMAN AVERAGES

First Experiment

NOTE.—The control sections are starred wherever they appear in Tables 1 through 8.

Senior A Class *	Mean ± Probable Error	Sigma	Sigma of the Mean	Mean ± Probable Error	Sigma	Sigma of the Mean
	OTIS SCORES			CHRONOLOGICAL AGE		
5 *........	46.42 ± 1.14	9.74	1.69	239.38 ± 1.37	11.75	2.05
7..........	51.13 ± .85	6.98	1.27	240.67 ± 1.12	9.58	1.67
8..........	50.82 ± .91	7.95	1.36	236.95 ± 1.21	10.40	1.81
9 *........	47.68 ± 1.00	8.72	1.50	235.91 ± 1.45	12.65	2.17
10..........	45.41 ± .80	6.93	1.19	237.82 ± 1.39	12.10	2.07
11 *........	47.77 ± .94	7.66	1.40	237.67 ± 1.43	11.74	2.14
12 *........	50.27 ± .95	7.54	1.41	239.16 ± .92	7.50	1.37
	PRACTICE GRADES			PERSONALITY TRAITS		
5 *........	4.50 ± .14	1.18	.21	36.66 ± .85	7.38	1.28
7..........	4.43 ± .18	1.46	.27	34.94 ± .88	7.22	1.32
8..........	4.35 ± .16	1.40	.24	36.72 ± .98	8.36	1.46
9 *........	4.21 ± .17	1.45	.25	34.18 ± 1.11	9.67	1.66
10..........	4.24 ± .14	1.25	.21	34.18 ± .95	8.28	1.42
11 *........	4.33 ± .14	1.13	.21	36.87 ± .86	7.09	1.29
12 *........	4.50 ± .15	1.27	.23	36.00 ± .90	7.36	1.34
	FRESHMAN AVERAGE					
5 *........	79.92 ± .35	2.99	.52			
7..........	81.97 ± .24	1.96	.36			
8..........	81.47 ± .33	2.80	.49			
9 *........	80.44 ± .32	2.78	.48			
10..........	79.97 ± .28	2.43	.42			
11 *........	81.50 ± .25	2.00	.37			
12 *........	81.97 ± .25	2.01	.37			

* Control Classes..............................5, 9, 11, 12
Experimental 8, 10
Double Experimental............................. 7

were the measures to be repeated the differences probably would
be in the same direction.

In both experiments the critical ratios of the freshman averages were consistently larger than the other equation bases.
No reliable explanation for this was forthcoming. It might

TABLE 2

SIGNIFICANCE OF DIFFERENCES IN CLASSIFICATION DATA AS SHOWN BY CRITICAL RATIOS OF DIFFERENCES BETWEEN AVERAGES

First Experiment

NOTE.—In order to find desired critical ratio of any two groups, select the column in which one group occurs and the row in which the second group occurs, and the block common to both will yield the correct critical ratio. When a critical ratio does not favor class listed at head of column a minus sign (−) has been placed before it.

Senior A Class *	OTIS SCORES					
	7	8	9 *	10	11 *	12 *
5 *...............	3.33	3.03	.84	− .74	.92	2.61
7................	....	− .25	− 2.64	− 4.94	− 2.67	− .68
8................	....	....	− 2.33	− 4.49	− 2.34	− .42
9 *...............	....	....	....	− 1.79	.06	1.89
10...............	....	....	....	....	1.92	3.95
11 *...............	....	....	....	....	....	1.89

	CHRONOLOGICAL AGE					
	7	8	9 *	10	11 *	12 *
5 *...............	.74	− 1.34	− 1.74	− .81	− .87	− .14
7................	....	− 2.27	− 2.61	− 1.61	− 1.67	− 1.05
8................	....	....	− .56	.48	.39	1.46
9 *...............	....	....	....	.96	.87	1.89
10...............	....	....	....	....	− .08	.81
11 *...............	....	....	....	....	....	.89

	PRACTICE GRADES					
	7	8	9 *	10	11 *	12 *
5 *...............	− .32	− .76	− 1.32	− 1.31	− .86	.00
7................	....	− .33	− .89	− .84	− .44	.30
8................	....	....	− .60	− .51	− .09	.68
9 *...............	....	....	....	.14	.54	1.28
10...............	....	....	....	....	.45	1.26
11 *...............	....	....	....	....	....	.83

	PERSONALITY TRAITS					
	7	8	9 *	10	11 *	12 *
5 *...............	− 1.40	.05	− 1.77	− 1.95	.18	− .54
7................	....	1.35	− .54	− .59	1.56	.84
8................	....	....	− 1.73	− 1.88	.12	.54
9 *...............	....	....	....	.00	1.92	1.28
10...............	....	....	....	....	2.10	1.40
11 *...............	....	....	....	....	....	− .71

TABLE 2 (*Continued*)

	FRESHMAN AVERAGES					
	7	8	9 *	10	11 *	12 *
5 *...............	4.88	3.27	1.10	.11	3.71	4.80
7...............	....	−1.23	− 3.83	− 5.46	− 1.35	.00
8...............	....	....	− 2.24	− 3.47	.08	1.23
9 *...............	....	....	....	− 1.10	2.61	3.77
10...............	....	....	....	....	4.10	5.37
11*...............	....	....	....	....	....	1.35

* Control Classes...........................5, 9, 11, 12
Experimental...............................8, 10
Double Experimental.......................... 7
* The critical ratio is the ratio of the difference in averages of any two groups on any item to the probable error of the difference on the item.   Unless the critical ratio is as much as 3 the difference may be due to chance.

TABLE 3

CLASSIFICATION OF GROUPS BY AVERAGES ON BASIS OF OTIS SCORES, CHRONOLOGICAL AGE, PRACTICE GROUPS, PERSONALITY RATINGS, AND FRESHMAN AVERAGES

Second Experiment

Senior A Class *	Mean ± Probable Error	Sigma	Sigma of the Mean	Mean ± Probable Error	Sigma	Sigma of the Mean
	OTIS SCORES			CHRONOLOGICAL AGE		
5..........	51.37 ± .67	5.42	1.01	236.81 ± 1.37	10.96	2.04
6..........	49.63 ± 1.12	9.30	1.67	236.50 ± 1.70	13.93	2.54
7 *........	46.92 ± .91	6.79	1.36	240.50 ± 1.34	10.00	2.00
8 *........	50.57 ± 1.21	9.57	1.81	239.82 ± 2.18	7.24	3.26
9..........	47.20 ± .91	6.77	1.36	240.90 ± 1.66	12.39	2.48
10 *........	53.55 ± 1.31	9.19	1.96	234.64 ± 1.61	11.28	2.40
	PRACTICE GRADES			PERSONALITY RATINGS		
5..........	4.29 ± .17	1.40	.26	33.86 ± .87	7.07	1.31
6..........	4.50 ± .16	1.29	.24	36.33 ± .82	6.73	1.23
7 *........	3.90 ± .17	1.30	.26	32.40 ± .87	6.52	1.30
8 *........	4.54 ± .20	1.59	.30	35.86 ± 1.02	8.12	1.53
9..........	4.42 ± .17	1.26	.25	33.60 ± 1.25	9.30	1.86
10 *........	4.36 ± .23	1.60	.34	33.00 ± 1.45	10.12	2.16
	FRESHMAN GRADES					
5..........	81.33 ± .29	2.38	.44			
6..........	81.27 ± .36	2.94	.54			
7 *........	79.06 ± .27	2.00	.40			
8 *........	79.39 ± .27	2.16	.41			
9..........	79.62 ± .38	2.82	.56			
10 *........	79.77 ± .44	3.08	.66			

* Control Classes............................7, 8, 10
Experimental.................................. 5, 9
Double Experimental.......................... 6

TABLE 4

SIGNIFICANCE OF DIFFERENCES IN CLASSIFICATION DATA AS SHOWN BY CRITICAL RATIOS OF DIFFERENCES BETWEEN AVERAGES

Second Experiment

NOTE.—In order to find desired critical ratio of any two groups, select the column in which one group occurs and the row in which the second group occurs, and the block common to both will yield the correct critical ratio. When C. R. does not "favor" class listed · at head of column a minus sign (−) has been placed before it.

Senior A Class *	OTIS SCORES				
	6	7 *	8 *	9	10 *
5............................	− 1.34	− 3.95	− .59	− 3.71	1.49
6............................	....	− 1.89	.57	− 1.70	2.31
7 *............................	....	....	2.42	.23	4.19
8 *............................	....	....	....	− 2.24	1.68
9............................	....	....	....	....	4.01

Senior A Class *	CHRONOLOGICAL AGE				
	6	7 *	8 *	9	10 *
5............................	− .15	1.94	1.17	1.91	3.26
6............................	....	1.86	1.20	1.86	1.35
7 *............................	....	....	− .27	.18	1.52
8 *............................	....	....	....	.39	1.41
9............................	....	....	....	....	1.19

Senior A Class *	PRACTICE GRADES				
	6	7 *	8 *	9	10 *
5............................	.90	− 1.58	.95	.54	.24
6............................	....	− 2.57	.17	− .35	− .49
7 *............................	....	....	2.40	2.16	1.61
8 *............................	....	....	....	− .48	− .60
9............................	....	....	....	....	− .29

Senior A Class *	PERSONALITY TRAITS				
	6	7 *	8 *	9	10 *
5............................	2.06	− 1.19	1.50	− .17	− 3.80
6............................	....	− 3.33	− .36	− 1.83	− 2.01
7 *............................	....	....	2.43	.80	.36
8 *............................	....	....	....	− 1.41	− 1.62
9............................	....	....	....	....	− .32

TABLE 4 (*Continued*)

	FRESHMAN GRADES				
	6	7 *	8 *	9	10 *
5...........................	− .14	− 5.78	− 4.85	− 3.62	− 2.96
6...........................	....	− 4.95	− 4.14	− 3.18	− 2.64
7 *........................	....	....	.87	1.22	1.38
8 *........................	....	....	....	.50	.74
9...........................	....	....	....	....	.26

* Control Classes.............................7, 8, 10
  Experimental................................. 5, 9
  Double Experimental.......................... 6

* The critical ratio is the ratio of the difference in the averages of any two groups of any item to the probable error of the difference of the item.   Unless the critical ratio is as much as 3 the difference may be due to chance.

have been that these students had not become oriented, or that the number of instructors grading, and the differences in their standards, influenced the results.   It will be seen that the objective test evidence, another pedagogical measure, does not show these large differences.   Were the experiment to be repeated, it might be better to eliminate freshman averages as a base.

Table 5 shows the distribution of objective test scores for the first experiment.   Table 6 presents the significance of differences between averages of objective test scores.   Table 7 gives the distribution of objective test scores for the second experiment, and Table 8 the significance of differences between objective test scores for that experiment.

INTERPRETATION OF OBJECTIVE TEST RESULTS AS SHOWN BY CRITICAL RATIOS

Individual Experimental Classes

First Experiment: SA[7] (double experimental) [6] from sixteen possible comparisons with individual control classes showed 11 comparisons where the chances are 1 to 22 and greater that the true difference can be as small as zero.   Of the remaining 5 possibilities ($3 \times$ P.E. $_{\text{diff. of the mean}}$) or more, 2 were in favor of SA[7] and 3 against.

In 80 per cent of the comparisons, SA[7], as far as the above data indicate, did at least as well as the control classes.

[6] "Double experimental" refers to that class in each experiment that had two small-group periods a week and one class period.   "Single experimental" classes had one small-group period a week and two class periods.   SA[5], SA[7] (Senior A[5], Senior A[7])

TABLE 5

DISTRIBUTION OF OBJECTIVE TEST SCORES BY AVERAGES

First Experiment

Senior A Class *	EXAMINATION 1			EXAMINATION 2		
	EXAMINATION—OCTOBER			EXAMINATION—NOVEMBER		
	Mean ± Probable Error	Sigma	Sigma of the Mean	Mean ± Probable Error	Sigma	Sigma of the Mean
5 *........	44.05 ± 1.16	9.97	1.73	37.88 ± 1.27	10.85	1.89
7..........	46.50 ± 1.28	10.49	1.91	38.27 ± 1.05	8.57	1.57
8..........	46.86 ± .93	8.03	1.40	40.79 ± .90	7.72	1.34
9 *........	46.21 ± 1.05	9.09	1.56	42.47 ± 1.13	9.83	1.69
10..........	44.97 ± .94	8.21	1.41	40.35 ± 1.51	13.16	2.26
11 *........	40.80 ± .95	7.77	1.42	44.27 ± .93	7.64	1.39
12 *........	49.20 ± 1.08	8.82	1.61	43.33 ± .93	7.61	1.39

Senior A Class *	EXAMINATION 3			FINAL EXAMINATION		
	EXAMINATION—DECEMBER					
	Mean ± Probable Error	Sigma	Sigma of the Mean	Mean ± Probable Error	Sigma	Sigma of the Mean
5 *........	44.30 ± 1.20	10.28	1.79	49.37 ± .36	3.09	.54
7..........	44.93 ± 1.21	9.90	1.81	51.20 ± .46	3.74	.68
8..........	40.91 ± .82	7.05	1.23	52.15 ± .38	3.19	.56
9 *........	42.47 ± 1.30	11.30	1.94	51.18 ± .33	2.93	.50
10..........	44.00 ± 1.18	10.28	1.76	53.35 ± .32	2.81	.48
11 *........	51.33 ± .86	7.04	1.29	51.53 ± .40	3.22	.59
12 *........	41.33 ± 1.15	9.36	1.71	51.27 ± .42	3.42	.62

```
* Control Classes........................5, 9, 11, 12
  Experimental...............................8, 10
  Double Experimental........................  7
```

SA[8] (single experimental) duplicated SA[7]'s record in comparisons recorded (.81 per cent).

SA[10] (single experimental) showed 7 comparisons where chances are 1 to 22 or greater that difference may be due to chance, and of the remaining 9 possibilities 6 were in favor of this class and 3 against.

TABLE 6
Significance of Differences Between Averages of Objective Test Scores as Shown by Critical Ratios *

First Experiment

Note.—In order to find desired Critical Ratio of any two groups, select the column in which one group occurs and the row in which the second group occurs and the block common to both will yield the correct critical ratio. When C. R. does not "favor" class listed at head of column a minus sign (−) has been placed before it.

Senior A Class *	EXAMINATION 1 (OBJECTIVE EXAMINATION)					
	7	8	9 *	10	11 *	12 *
5 *..............	1.43	1.89	1.40	.62	− 2.18	3.27
7..............	....	.23	− .18	− .98	− 3.59	1.62
8..............	....	....	− .47	− 1.43	− 4.58	1.65
9 *..............	....	....	....	− .89	− 3.84	2.0
10..............	....	....	....	....	− 3.14	2.97
11 *..............	....	....	....	....	....	5.79

	EXAMINATION 2 (NOVEMBER EXAMINATION)					
	7	8	9 *	10	11 *	12 *
5 *..............	.24	1.88	2.78	1.26	4.31	3.66
7..............	....	1.83	2.81	1.14	4.59	3.87
8..............	....	....	1.20	− .26	2.91	2.13
9 *..............	....	....	....	− 1.16	1.35	1.65
10..............	....	....	....	....	2.31	1.76
11 *..............	....	....	....	....	....	− .84

	EXAMINATION 3 (DECEMBER EXAMINATION)					
	7	8	9 *	10	11 *	12 *
5 *..............	.38	− 2.34	− 1.04	− .18	4.77	− 1.80
7..............	....	2.76	− 1.40	− .56	4.32	− 2.21
8..............	....	....	1.02	2.16	8.78	.30
9 *..............	....	....	....	.83	5.70	− .66
10..............	....	....	....	....	5.04	− 1.64
11 *..............	....	....	....	....	....	− 7.01

	FINAL EXAMINATION					
	7	8	9 *	10	11 *	12 *
5 *..............	3.15	5.34	3.68	8.30	4.05	3.47
7..............	....	1.62	− .03	3.89	.56	.12
8..............	....	....	− 1.94	2.43	− 1.16	− 1.58
9 *..............	....	....	....	4.71	.68	.17
10..............	....	....	....	....	− 3.59	− 4.01
11 *..............	....	....	....	....	....	− .45

* Control Classes...........................5, 9, 11, 12
Experimental................................8, 10
Double Experimental..........................7

* The critical ratio is the ratio of the differences in the averages of any two groups on any item to the probable error of the difference on the item. Unless the critical ratio is as much as 3 the difference may be due to chance.

TABLE 7

DISTRIBUTION OF OBJECTIVE TEST SCORES BY AVERAGES

Second Experiment

Senior A Class *	OBJECTIVE EXAMINATION 1			OBJECTIVE EXAMINATION 2		
	Mean ± Probable Error	Sigma	Sigma of the Mean	Mean ± Probable Error	Sigma	Sigma of the Mean
5..........	54.74 ± .98	7.94	1.47	68.78 ± 1.21	9.70	1.80
6..........	45.10 ± 2.37	11.21	3.54	71.20 ± 1.21	9.84	1.80
7*.........	42.46 ± 1.31	9.74	1.95	61.10 ± 1.54	11.48	2.30
8*.........	45.79 ± 1.63	12.84	2.43	68.86 ± 1.12	8.80	1.66
9..........	44.62 ± 1.43	10.65	2.13	67.46 ± 1.62	12.08	2.42
10*.........	47.91 ± 1.60	11.20	2.39	69.09 ± 1.65	11.58	2.46

Senior A Class *	OBJECTIVE EXAMINATION 3			FINAL EXAMINATION		
	Mean ± Probable Error	Sigma	Sigma of the Mean	Mean ± Probable Error	Sigma	Sigma of the Mean
5..........	59.22 ± 1.41	11.38	2.11	78.29 ± .54	4.38	.81
6..........	56.30 ± 1.47	11.97	2.19	75.60 ± .77	6.32	1.15
7*.........	53.94 ± 1.09	8.14	1.63	74.06 ± .66	4.92	.98
8*.........	57.43 ± 1.23	9.66	1.83	76.25 ± .48	3.81	.72
9..........	55.50 ± 1.54	11.48	2.30	77.78 ± .68	5.11	1.02
10*.........	56.32 ± 2.22	15.57	3.32	78.09 ± .89	6.23	1.33

```
* Control Classes............................7, 8, 10
  Experimental................................. 5, 9
  Double Experimental.........................   6
```

Second Experiment: SA[6] (double experimental) from 12 possible comparisons [7] with individual control classes showed 11 comparisons where the chances are 1 to 22 and greater that the true difference can be as small as zero and therefore probably due to chance. The remaining possibility favored SA[6].

In 91 per cent of the comparisons SA[6], as far as the above data are indicative, did at least as well as the control groups.

SA[5] (single experimental) from 12 possible comparisons showed 7 comparisons where the chances are 1 to 22 or greater that the true difference can be as small as zero. Of the remaining five

---

[7] Six instead of seven classes participated in the second experiment.

TABLE 8

Significance of Differences Between Averages of Objective Test Scores as Shown by Critical Ratios *

Second Experiment

Note.—In order to find desired critical ratio of any two groups, select the column in which one group occurs and the row in which the second group occurs and the block common to both will yield the correct critical ratio. When C. R. does not "favor" class listed at head of column a minus sign (−) has been placed before it.

Senior A Class *	Objective Examination—1				
	6	7 *	8 *	9	10 *
5.............................	− 3.78	− 7.53	− 4.73	− 5.40	− 3.70
6.............................	....	− .98	.24	− .18	.99
7 *............................	....	....	1.61	1.10	4.62
8 *............................	....	....	....	− .54	.93
9.............................	....	....	....	....	1.55

	Objective Examination—2				
	6	7 *	8 *	9	10 *
5.............................	1.43	− 4.0	.05	− .66	.15
6.............................	....	− 5.24	− 1.44	− 1.86	− 1.04
7 *............................	....	....	4.11	2.85	3.56
8 *............................	....	....	....	− .72	.12
9.............................	....	....	....	....	.71

	Objective Examination—3				
	6	7 *	8 *	9	10 *
5.............................	− 1.44	− 2.96	− .96	− 1.79	− 1.11
6.............................	....	− 1.29	.59	− .24	.02
7 *............................	....	....	2.13	.83	.96
8 *............................	....	....	....	− .99	− .44
9.............................	....	....	....	....	.30

	Final Examination				
	6	7 *	8 *	9	10 *
5.............................	− 2.87	5.00	− 2.84	− .59	− .20
6.............................	....	− 1.53	.72	2.13	2.13
7 *............................	....	....	2.72	3.96	3.70
8 *............................	....	....	....	1.83	1.83
9.............................	....	....	....	....	.29

```
* Control Classes.............................7, 8, 10
  Experimental................................. 5, 9
  Double Experimental......................... 6
```

* The critical ratio is the ratio of the difference in the averages of any two groups on any item to the probable error of the difference on the item. Unless the critical ratio is as much as 3 the difference may be due to chance.

possibilities all favored SA[5].   In 58 per cent of the comparisons SA[5] did at least as well as the control groups.

SA[9] (single experimental) from 12 possible comparisons showed 11 comparisons where the chances are 1 to 21 and greater that the true difference can be as small as zero.   The remaining possibility (3 × P.E. $_{\text{diff. of mean}}$) favored SA[9].[8]

Total Control Group and Total Experimental Group

Because of the small number of students in the individual classes, it seemed best to compare, in each experiment, the test performance of the total control group with that of the total experimental group.[9]   *Two* methods of combining classes were used:

1. One method turned the individual raw scores into standard scores by finding each student's individual deviation from the mean score of each examination and dividing that deviation by the standard deviation for that examination.

   Steps:

   (*a*)[10] Student's standard score for examination 1 =
   $$\frac{\text{Mean (c + e)}_{\text{ex.1}} - \text{Individual raw score}_{\text{ex.1}}}{\text{sigma}_{(c+e)}}$$

   (*b*)   Student's standard score on three examinations =
   St. sc. 1 + st. sc. 2 + st. sc. 3 [11]

   (*c*)   Frequency distribution of standard scores of control group and experimental group.

   (*d*)   Find mean and standard deviation of each.

   (*e*)   Compare these means by critical ratio techniques.

The results of the measures recorded in Table 9 warrant the conclusion that in Experiment 1 there was a rather strong tendency in favor of the control method, but the difference of the means; was not 3 × P.E. $_{\text{diff. of mean}}$.   In the second experiment there is very strong evidence in favor of the experimental method but again the critical ratio is not 3 or more.

---

[8] If further interpretations in terms of chances are desired attention is called to Diagram, Appendix D.

[9] In Experiment 1 there were 127 control students and 97 experimental ones; in Experiment 2 there were 75 control and 84 experimental ones.

[10] Examinations 2 and 3 were treated in same manner.   Final examinations were treated separately.

[11] No averaging was done because there was no interest in individual scores as such.

Table 9 gives comparison of averages on examinations 1, 2, and 3 by use of critical ratios based on standard scores.

TABLE 9

COMPARISON OF AVERAGES ON EXAMINATIONS 1, 2, AND 3, BY USE OF CRITICAL
RATIOS BASED ON STANDARD SCORES

First Experiment

Group	Mean ± P.E.	Standard Deviation	Difference of Means	Critical Ratio
Control Group..............	+ .09 ± .112	1.87 ⎫	.39 ± .171	2.29
Experimental Group.........	− .29 ± .129	1.88 ⎬ '		

Second Experiment

Group	Mean ± P.E.	Standard Deviation	Difference of Means	Critical Ratio
Control Group..............	− .35 ± .163	2.10 ⎫	.66 ± .227	2.90
Experimental Group........,..	+ .30 ± .158	2.15 ⎬		

2. Because of the tendency of the "standard" technique to draw the means toward the zero point a second comparison of the total control group with the total experimental group was made. This time the comparison was based on raw scores to make certain that the *technique* did not force the small difference. The mean and the standard deviation of the raw scores of the combined control group and the combined experimental group were computed.

The results of the measures recorded in Table 10 again show critical ratios of less than 3 and warrant the same conclusion as warranted by those in Table 9; namely, that the differences may be due to chance and that there is probability that the true difference may be as small as zero.

It will be noted that no mention has been made of the results of the final examination.[12] These results were not combined with those of the other examinations because of the low correlation

[12] It will be remembered that this examination was formulated by all instructors teaching this subject and by the head of the department of psychology and education.

$(+ .23)$ between them. These results, therefore, offer another measure of comparison.

Table 10 shows the comparison of averages on examinations 1, 2, and 3 by use of critical ratios based on raw scores.

TABLE 10

COMPARISON OF AVERAGES ON EXAMINATIONS 1, 2, AND 3 BY USE OF CRITICAL RATIOS BASED ON RAW SCORES *

First Experiment

	Mean ± P.E.	Standard Deviation	Difference of Means	Critical Ratio
Control Group...............	128.6 ± 1.129	18.86 ⎫	2.5 ± 1.68	1.49
Experimental Group.........	126.1 ± 1.248	18.22 ⎭		

Second Experiment

	Mean ± P.E.	Standard Deviation	Difference of Means	Critical Ratio
Control Group...............	166.9 ± 1.814	23.29 ⎫	6.9 ± 2.57	2.68
Experimental Group.........	173.8 ± 1.825	24.80 ⎭		

* Left unaveraged because interest did not lie in individual scores.

TABLE 11

COMPARISON OF AVERAGES ON FINAL EXAMINATION BY USE OF MEANS AND CRITICAL RATIOS OF STANDARD SCORES *

First Experiment

	Mean ± P.E.	Standard Deviation	Difference of Means	Critical Ratio
Control Group...............	− .185 ± .059	.984 ⎫	.462 ± .091	5.08
Experimental Group.........	+ .267 ± .069	1.009 ⎭		

Second Experiment

	Mean ± P.E.	Standard Deviation	Difference of Means	Critical Ratio
Control Group...............	− .138 ± .076	.974 ⎫	.021 ± .106	1.98
Experimental Group.........	− .159 ± .074	1.006 ⎭		

* Left unaveraged.

Examination of Tables 11 and 12 reveals evidence that in the final or departmental examination the experimental group did at least as well as the control group in the second experiment and decidedly better than in the first experiment.

Table 12 gives the comparison of averages on final examination by use of critical ratios based on raw scores.

TABLE 12

COMPARISON OF AVERAGES ON FINAL EXAMINATION BY USE OF CRITICAL
RATIOS BASED ON RAW SCORES

First Experiment

	Mean $\pm$ P.E.	Standard Deviation	Difference of Means	Critical Ratio
Control Group...............	50.4 $\pm$ .191	3.19 ⎫	1.5 $\pm$ .296	5.07
Experimental Group..........	51.9 $\pm$ .226	3.30 ⎭		

Second Experiment

Control Group...............	75.69 $\pm$ .412	5.294 ⎫	1.26 $\pm$ .578	2.18
Experimental Group..........	76.95 $\pm$ .404	5.497 ⎭		

CONCLUSION

The statistical evidence throughout the experiment leads to the following conclusion: The experimental group did at least as well as the control group as evidenced by the objective test results, and the data tend to favor slightly the experimental method.

CHAPTER IV

SUBJECTIVE JUDGMENTS OF THE EXPERIMENTAL PERIOD

What may be said of the factors in this study that could not be measured quantitatively?

Without doubt instructors studying in the small-group study-discussion procedure would be interested in the evaluation that the students made of this period, in whether they liked it or not, and in what they felt they got or failed to get. Interest might be evinced also in the instructor's observations, although his judgments would of necessity be of a subjective nature. As yet science has invented no absolutely reliable quantitative measuring instrument for the weighing of factors such as these—the concomitant or by-product learnings, possibilities always present in a real learning-teaching situation. In these concomitant values, as facilitating instruments of aid in life adjustments, many educational leaders place as much faith, and at times even more, than in the primary learnings, in this case the possession of those facts tested in the objective examinations.

In this situation the only subjective judgments available were those of the students and the instructor participating in the experiment.

Several possible procedures of arriving at these judgments were considered, but all but one had to be abandoned. The classes and instructor participating in the experiment were merely a small cross-section of a large city school with all its elaborate machinery. Permission to carry on the experiment at all was granted only upon condition that the organization be disturbed in no way. The daily routine made it impossible to bring in judges from the outside with the exception of the head of the department and the principal of the school. The instructor was granted the privilege of teaching just one subject for two terms, which privilege made it possible to gather the data in a single year and to have enough cases to make the findings statistically reliable.

It was finally decided to ask for anonymous statements from those students participating in the small-group period. They were asked to state in their own words whether or not they liked the small-group period and, if possible, to support their opinions with reasons. They were invited to make suggestions if they cared to do so. No list was given to these students to be checked lest the responses be influenced by the suggestions offered. To further insure absolute freedom of expression these statements were not asked for until the students knew their term grades had been filed in the administrative offices.

The opinions were read and classified by a jury (an administrator, a psychologist, a critic teacher, an instructor, and a layman).

These opinions were organized in two ways—first, "for" the period, "against" the period, and "for and against"; secondly, according to frequency of reasons advanced "for" and "against." Statements were classified as adverse when from their wording they seemed to indicate the student's intention, although at times a student's opinion in the eyes of the judges might have been rated "for" instead of "against" because the factors mentioned seemed to be aspects of strength instead of weakness.[1]

RESULTS OF STUDENT OPINION
OF EXPERIMENTAL PERIOD

	Per Cent
For	58.55
Against	10.6
For, with suggestions for improvement of procedure	30.85

According to the judges, the greater majority (about 88 per cent) wanted and liked the small-group study-discussion period. The reasons advanced were difficult to classify, for, although the same reason appeared again and again, it was differently worded each time. Many indicated personal values that were not duplicated by other students.[2]

These statements seemed sincere, and likes, dislikes, and reasons were expressed in no uncertain terms. So forthright were many of them as to be quite vehement, and in spots they were unintentionally humorous.

[1] Quotation from a statement: "I think this period was a failure because we argued too much and so seldom entirely agreed."
[2] See Appendix for sample quotations with exact wording from these statements.

Among reasons most frequently advanced for liking this type of period were, in effect, that: [3]

a) It cuts down homework.

b) It affords easy access to the reference material not available in public libraries, or only obtainable after a long period of waiting.

c) It makes it "easier" to speak in the larger group.

d) Points discussed are clearer after the small-group discussions.

e) It broadens one's viewpoints to hear those of others.

f) Every girl has an opportunity to express her opinion in the small groups.

g) There is the opportunity to become familiar with all the reference material when there is too much for one alone to read.

h) It helps us to distinguish what is important and what is not.

i) It is a great help to the poorer students.

The following are some of the arguments advanced by the students who said they did not like the small-group study plan:

a) Some girls did all the work and those who were not sincere received what was said uncritically.

b) Time was wasted in talking of things other than the material of the course.

c) Too much time was wasted in arguing.

d) The group covered too little ground.

e) It became a library or reading period.

f) It gave opportunity for so many expressions of personal opinion that we could not decide upon *one* answer for a question.

These statements yield two more important points of evidence. Some students stated that they would like to have been allowed to do reading at home as well as during the period set aside for this purpose.[4] Ordinarily, voluntary extra-mural reading on the part of the students would be stimulated.

The statements in general seemed to yield decided evidence that the technique of conducting these small-group periods needed improvement. It will be remembered that the instructor had

---

[3] The students' own wording is preserved as nearly as possible even in this summary.

[4] It is readily recognized that these statements belonged to members of those groups having two experimental periods a week.

offered no suggestions during the experiment as to how these small groups should proceed.   Various suggestions for improving their procedure technique were made.[5]

The anonymous statements yielded the following suggestions as possibilities for improving the small-group procedure:

a) That the leader should be held responsible for seeing that all in the group share the work.

b) That the groups have a different leader each time.

c) That a check-up be made at the end of each period and thus prevent "side discussions."

d) That the instructor definitely plan the procedure for all the groups.

e) That the group give its time to individual reading and study and not take time to discuss the references.

f) That frequent changes be made in the groups.

g) That chairmen should prevent a few in group from dominating discussions.

h) That the groups be kept more nearly together in the amount of work covered.

i) That the first half of each of the three periods of the week be given to small-group discussion and the latter half to class discussion.

j) That they be allowed to take home for more intensive reading reference books which particularly appealed to them.[6]

The reader will readily see that some of these suggestions have real value while others apparently have not.   For instance, since the entire term offers only about forty-five periods in all it would not be feasible or practical to change the personnel of the groups, because that would necessitate another orientation of personalities, and because each member of the new group might be working on widely divergent parts of the course (each group moved at its own rate of speed).

---

[5] In the eight months that have elapsed since the close of the experiment the author has been gathering evidence as to various procedures for the small-group period, but of course this could not be included in the present study.

[6] The reference material was not taken from the classroom during the period of experimentation.

THE INSTRUCTOR'S OBSERVATIONS

The entire experiment could be looked at from another point of view—what the author herself, as instructor of the course in principles of education, observed as the experiment progressed. From time to time the following observations were made and noted. They seem to be observable evidence of the value of the experimental procedure. The reader is left to make his own evaluation of them.

1. During the regular class discussions it was an unusual occurrence to find any member of the experimental groups unprepared for the day's assignment.
2. Entirely inaccurate or extraneous material seemed to have been eliminated in the small-group discussions. This economized class time.
3. These students handled the reference materials with ease and became increasingly adept in using them to support and make more authoritative their own opinions.
4. Every one of these students, either through his own reading or through listening to members of his small group, had had contacts with *all* the suggested reference materials.
5. There was a lack of tension in these classes both before and during the regular class discussions.
6. The nodding of heads, smiles, and an "I-told-you-so" shaking of fingers exchanged between members of a discussion group when a question was settled in the class seemed to indicate that the group had come into class with differences of opinion and an interest in the outcome.
7. The discussions in these classes were more animated and individual opinions more authoritatively held.
8. There seemed to be a tendency in these groups, when they did not settle an argument to their own satisfaction, even with the instructor's help, to carry it outside the class and to seek other sources of authority (teachers, parents, friends, books, etc.).
9. Those classes not having this small-group period made a strong appeal to have one and were not at all satisfied when told that since the period was only being tried out experi-

mentally it would not be wise to expose all classes to it until some evidence had been gathered.

10. These students seemed able to handle controversial issues of a more or less personal nature (religion, morals, family adjustments, etc.) with tolerance, little animosity, and less vehemence even when they had to agree to disagree.

11. Words like the following were frequently heard—"Well, I've always believed or thought . . . but I guess I'll have to change my mind on that point if I'm going to be sensible!"

12. Of course, beyond the readily observable fact that these students spoke from seemingly broader points of view, answered more frequently with less emotional bias, and the like, only the student herself could really know whether or not there actually had been a change in her points of view and a more careful formulation of new ones.

CONCLUSIONS

The following conclusions may be drawn from the students' opinions concerning the small-group discussion-study periods. On the whole, the students were found to favor these periods, and considered them helpful in many ways. Careful analysis of the statements of those students who said they disliked the discussion periods indicates a dissatisfaction, not so much with the type of period as with some features of the procedure of their particular groups. In general, these students expressed the opinion that the small-group procedure could be improved, and they made suggestions to that effect.

CHAPTER V

CONCLUSIONS AND RECOMMENDATIONS

THE PROBLEM AGAIN

Did the use of carefully selected reference material and the small-group study-discussion periods reduce required extra-class study appreciably, yield concomitants of value, and yet enable the students to achieve as good results in their examinations as if all the class periods had been given to class discussion?

CONCLUSIONS

The statistical computations show definitely that the students who had the small-group study-discussion procedure, considered as classes and as an entire group, did at least as well in the three intra-term tests as the control students.

In the final examination the experimental group made even a better showing than in the other three examinations.

There seemed to be little or no difference between the results achieved by the double experimental group and the single one, making purely optional, or dependent upon factors not shown in this study, whether the proportionate use of this period shall be one or two out of three class periods.

The use of this period eliminated required extra-class study entirely for the classes having two of the small-group periods a week, and radically lessened it for those having one of these periods a week, inasmuch as they read only the one text and not always that outside the class period.

Student judgment favored the use of the small-group period, and found it rich in personal values, but may be said to have indicated that various specific techniques as to its working procedure might enhance its concomitant values and make its direct outcomes more certain.

Therefore, it may be reliably stated that the use of this type of period is not only justified from a statistical evaluation of direct results as shown by the objective test evidence, but also from the fact that it stimulates and affords possibilities for the development of some of those concomitants which are of great value in adjusting satisfactorily to any type of social situation.

RECOMMENDATIONS

This study is limited in its scope and offers only a small contribution to possibilities of method procedures on the college level. Perhaps its greatest value lies not in what it has proved but in opening the way for further research.

There seems to be a decided need at present for almost exact repetition of some of the method studies already made. Each experiment has so many, and so entirely different, variables that at present it is impossible to compare results or evaluate transfer possibilities with any dependability. More proof is needed to confirm or refute the claims of studies already made of teaching methods on upper levels. So far as the writer could judge from an intensive analysis of studies already made, her own included, there is not enough evidence on any one method to warrant its unquestioned adoption or use without further experimentation. Of course this needed piling up of reliable evidence is extremely difficult. Universities at present tend to frown on mere repetition of research studies already made and advise against studies in methods, or even principles of methods, when research students are working in any field above the elementary school level. These institutions urge originality of research which in this field of method at this particular time may be ill-advised if those college teachers more interested in the art of teaching, and in the scientific phases already established, and not in experimentation, are to have practical, reliable help in improving their classroom methods of instruction. In the elementary school field sufficient studies have been made in certain method fields to enable a teacher to adopt not one best method—there is no such thing, nor would it probably be desirable—but to have decidedly reliable guides in selecting and arranging method procedures. Very little such help is available for the college instructor and is sorely needed and desired by those who do not rest serenely in the belief in their own teaching methods and who would like to try different ones.

Some questions suggested by this study, answers to which would prove helpful in the field of methods on the college level, are as follows:

1. Might there be one or two particular procedures for the small-group work that would yield better results than if the groups were, as in this study, left to arrange their own procedure?

2. In what way do the personal attributes of an instructor and his attitude toward a method influence its effective use?

3. What would a comparative study of individual study and the small-group method show?

4. What would be the difference in results if the small groups were given no guidance by the instructor, guided as in this study when guidance was requested, or definitely be given so many minutes of the instructor's time each period?

5. In what other course or courses might there be possibilities of transfer of values which proved to be effective in this particular use of a general method technique?

6. Would the use of a general technique, such as this, over a continued period of time result in a growth of those abilities affected by such a procedure?

7. How would freshman students compare with senior students in ability to use this procedure?

8. Is it possible or desirable to evaluate statistically the concomitants inherent in this technique?

BIBLIOGRAPHY

BOOKS

BROOKS, R. C. *Reading for Honors at Swarthmore.* Oxford Univ. Press, 1927.

BURTON, W. H. *The Nature and Direction of Learning.* Appleton, 1929.

CHANDLER, P. *Some Methods of Teaching in Six Representative State Teachers Colleges of the United States.* Bureau of Publications, Teachers College, Columbia University, 1930.

DOUGLAS, HARL AND OTHERS. University of Oregon Publications, Vol. I, No. 7, Education Series, February, 1929.

GOOD, C. V. *Teaching in College and University.* Warwick and York, 1929.

GRAY, W. S., Editor. *The Training of College Teachers.* University of Chicago Press, 1930.

GWINN, C. W. *An Experimental Study of Classroom Teaching.* George Peabody College Contributions to Education, No. 76.

HUDELSON, EARL. *Problems of College Education.* University of Minnesota Press, 1928.

KENT, R. A. C., Editor. *Higher Education in America.* Ginn, 1930.

KILPATRICK, W. H. *Foundations of Method.* Macmillan, 1925.

KLAPPER, PAUL. *Contemporary Education.* Appleton, 1929.

McCONN, MAX. *College or Kindergarten.* Chapter VI: "How Should It Be Taught?" New Republic, Inc., 1929.

McGAUGHY, J. RALPH. *Fiscal Administration of City School Systems.* Publication of the Educational Finance Inquiry, Vol. V, 1924.

NATIONAL SOCIETY OF COLLEGE TEACHERS OF EDUCATION. *Eighteenth Yearbook.* 1929.

REEDER, E. "The Development of Study—An Historical Survey." Master's Thesis, 1924.

WAKEHAM, GLEN. *American Association of University Professors*, Vol. XVI, No. 5, May, 1930.

WILKINS, ERNEST H. *The Changing College.* University of Chicago Press, 1927.

PAMPHLETS AND MAGAZINES

BAKER, F. E. "How Teachers Colleges Improve Instruction." *Journal of the National Education Association*, 20: 87-8. March, 1931.

BANE, C. L. "The Lecture vs. the Class-Discussion Method of College Teaching." *School and Society*, 21. ꞏ ꞏ ꞏ ꞏ ꞏ March 7, 1925.

BREWSTER, ETHEL. "Reading for Honors at Swarthmore." *Journal of Higher Education*, 1: 507–14, December, 1930.

BROOKS, W. S. "Means of Improving College Teaching." *Education*, 51: 236–39, December, 1930.

CLUGSTON, H. A. AND DAVIS, R. A. "Suggested Criteria for the Philosophical Method of Research in Education." *Educational Administration and Supervision*, 16: 575–80, November, 1930.

COFFMAN, LOTUS D. "Criticism and Culture." *Journal of Home Economics*, 18: 560–68, October, 1926.

CRAWFORD, C. C. "Defects and Difficulties in College Teaching." *School, and Society*, 28: 497–502, October 27, 1928.

DEWEY, JOHN. "Construction and Criticism," the first Davies memorial lecture, delivered February 25, 1930, for the Institute of Arts and Sciences, New York.

DONOVAN, H. L. "Changing Conceptions of College Teaching." *Educational Administration and Supervision*, 16: 401–10, September, 1930.

EVENDEN, E. S. "Improvement of College Teaching." *Teachers College Record*, 29: 587–96, 1928.

GOOD, CARTER V. "Bibliography on College Teaching with Special Emphasis on Methods of Teaching." N. S. C. T. E. *Sixteenth Yearbook*, 1928.

GOOD, CARTER V. "Methods in Teacher-Training." *Journal of Higher Education*, 1: 391–95, 453–61, November, 1930.

GOOD, CARTER V. N. S. C. T. E. *Sixteenth Yearbook*, pp. 66–95, 1928.

GREENE, E. B. "The Relative Effectiveness of Lectures and Individual Reading as Methods." *Genetic Psychology Monographs*, IV: 459–563, December, 1928.

HAGGERTY, M. E. "Improving College Instruction." *School and Society*, 27: 25–37, January 14, 1928.

HUDELSON, EARL. "Survey of Investigations Using Quantitative Criteria in Evaluation of Teaching." N. S. C. T. E. *Eighteenth Yearbook*, 1929.

HUDELSON, EARL. "Are Classes too Large?" *Journal of Higher Education*, 1: 436–39, November, 1930.

KELLY, F. J. "Needed Research in Higher Education." N. S. C. T. E. *Educational Monographs*, 1925–26.

MINER, J. B. "A New Type of College Course." *School and Society*, 22: 416–22, October 3, 1925.

PARRISH, W. M. "Technique in Higher Education." *Educational Review*, 69: 225–30, May, 1925.

REEVES, F. W. AND RUSSELL, J. D. "Some Aspects of Current Efforts to Improve College Instruction." University of Kentucky, Vol. 1, December, 1928, No. 2.

ROGERS, L. B. "Desirable Standards for Doctor's Dissertation. Should Dissertation be Based on Other Forms in Addition to Research?" *Educational Administration and Supervision*, 16: 683–92, December, 1930.

ROSS, CLAY C. "Study Methods of College Students in Relation to Intelligence and Achievement." *Educational Administration and Supervision*, 13: 551–62, November, 1927.

SPENCE, R. B. "Lecture and Class Discussion in Teaching Educational Psychology." *Journal of Educational Psychology*, 19: 454–62, October, 1928.

TOOPS, H. AND NEWLAND, T. E., are compiling an exhaustive bibliography of titles pertinent to college and university problems (not yet published).

WILKINS, E. H. Quoted by E. L. Donovan. *Educational Administration and Supervision*, 16: 410, September, 1930.

WILLIS, H. E. "The Next Step in Higher Education." *School and Society*, 24: 217–26, August 21, 1926.

WOODRING, M. N. AND FLEMMING, C. W. "A Survey of Investigations on Study." *Teachers College Record*, 29: 527–49; 605–17, 1928–29.

WOODY AND OTHERS. "Quantitative Measures in Higher Learning." *Journal of Higher Education*, October, 1931.

WYCKOFF, G. S. "Improvement of Teaching." *School and Society*, 29: 58–59, January 12, 1929.

ZOOK, G. F. "Major Problems in the Improvement of Instruction in Higher Institutions." *School and Society*, 30: 277–82, August 31, 1929.

APPENDIX A

OUTLINE OF COURSE IN PRINCIPLES OF EDUCATION

I. Introduction

Discussion (no preparation on part of students) as to their ideas of what principles are, how formulated and how used. Illustrations drawn from all fields (science, philosophy, religion, etc.)

II. Meaning and Purposes of Education

Changes from Grecian times to present

Contributions of philosophy, science, art, and sociology

III. Aims of Education

A. Factors determining aims a country adopts or formulates

B. Varying historical emphases

C. Values and purposes

IV. Formal and Informal Education

A. Historical development

B. Advantages and disadvantages

C. Conflicting conceptions of purposes of formal education

D. Dewey's philosophy and educational theories

V. Life Adjustment and Education

A. Facility of adjustment now and in primitive times

B. Adjustments essential in modern world
   1. To the physical world
   2. To economic situations
   3. To family situations
   4. To social and civic situations

C. Resources facilitating adjustment and education's part in developing them
   1. Physical and mental health
   2. Recreation
   3. Ethics and religion
   4. Intellectual activities

VI. Man's Equipment for Learning

A. Native
   1. Biological factors
   2. Psychological factors
   3. Sociological factors

B. Acquired
   1. Habits

2. Language
3. Personalities
4. Reflective thinking
5. Appreciative attitudes

VII. ORGANIZATION OF FORMAL EDUCATION AND ITS INFLUENCES ON ADJUST-
MENT
    A. Curriculum or subject
    B. Methods of teaching
    C. Measurement possibilities
    D. Functions of various school levels
        1. Pre-school (nursery school)
        2. Lower elementary (kindergarten and grades 1 to 4)
        3. Upper elementary (grades 4 to 6, or 4 to 8)
        4. Secondary (high, or junior high and high)
        5. Higher levels (junior college, college, university)

REFERENCES USED BY STUDENTS

TEXTS

Thorndike and Gates	Elementary Principles of Education	Macmillan
Chapman and Counts	Principles of Education	Houghton Mifflin

REFERENCE READING

Allport	Social Psychology	Houghton Mifflin
Bode	Modern Educational Theories	Macmillan
Burton	The Nature and Direction of Learning	Appleton
Clow *	Principles of Sociology	Macmillan
Dewey	Democracy and Education	Macmillan
Dewey	How We Think	D. C. Heath
Frasier and Armentrout	An Introduction to Education	Scott, Foresman
Grizzell	Education: Principles and Practices	Macmillan
Jennings	Biological Bases of Human Nature	W. W. Norton
Kilpatrick	Source Book in Philosophy of Education	Macmillan
Kilpatrick	Foundations of Method	Macmillan
Klapper	Contemporary Education	Appleton
Kulp	Outlines of Sociology of Human Behavior	Bureau of Publications, Teachers College
Mossman	Teaching and Learning in the Upper Elementary School	Houghton Mifflin
Thomas	Principles of Education	Houghton Mifflin

* The text used in this institution for the course in Educational Sociology.

BOOK REPORTS MADE TO CLASSES BY INDIVIDUALS[1]

Lynd	Middletown
Dimnet	The Art of Thinking
Dewey	A Quest for Certainty
Counts	The American Road to Culture

SAMPLE SHEET FROM SYLLABUS USED BY STUDENTS: AIMS OF
EDUCATION [2]

TOPIC III

1. What factors determine the nature of "schooling" that a country offers its people?
2. Trace briefly some of the changing educational emphases from early Grecian times to the present. What effect have these purposes and aims had on the curricula and the organization of the schools?
3. What contributions have the schools of the past made to the schools of the present?
4. "Aims are less broad than purposes and are therefore more definite working grades." "A good aim must be helpful in deciding upon particular steps in educating effectively." In the light of these statements, formulate some general aim of education that will meet modern needs.
5. Why is it so essential that we, as teachers, have and keep constantly before us general and specific aims, or ultimate and immediate aims of education?

REFERENCES

Thorndike and		
Gates	Elementary Principles of Education	pp. 14–32
Grizzell	Educational Principles and Practices	pp. 1–17, 87,103
Klapper	Contemporary Education	pp. 1–25
Chapman and		
Counts	Principles of Education	p. XII
Dewey	Democracy and Education	pp. 121–129
Frasier and		
Armentrout	An Introduction to Education	pp. 323–342

[1] This list of books contained many other titles and was known as the "Optional Reading List." Students received credit for any of these books which they read and on which they wrote a report.

[2] There was a similar sample sheet for every major topic in the outline. It is to be remembered that these questions did not dominate the discussion but stimulated and in addition guided the reading. Many other questions were brought up by the instructor and the students.

APPENDIX B

QUOTATIONS FROM STUDENTS' ANONYMOUS STATEMENTS

"FOR"

"This is carrying out one of the foremost principles in the new system of education for we are having a real life situation in school."

"I work incessantly over school work and find that I give more time to one study than another. Afterwards I find I have given the wrong proportions. This work was consoling. The group helped me in deciding what was important."

"Frequently a student can explain something to another student better than a teacher can."

"Not a biased way of studying because many ideas are conflicting and it makes us think which we believe to be true."

"This plan gave us a chance to check our opinions by the teacher's."

"This gave us a chance to use books hard to get outside."

"I would like to see this period tried in other subjects."

"Everyone likes to voice an opinion and in the small group this was possible."

"Every girl had an opportunity to have her say."

"A student could not be unprepared unless she had been absent or asleep. The former possible, the latter impossible because our discussions were too exciting."

"This plan covers more reference material in less time as each girl usually took a reference and reported on it to the group."

"I feel I could now use supervised study in my teaching."

"I learned to weigh one authority against another."

"I feel this period does away with prejudice in talking of questions of religion, etc."

"The work in the small group gives me the assurance to volunteer speaking in the larger group."

"It certainly cut out a lot of homework."

"The discussion in our group helped us to combine our viewpoints into one good concept."

"It gives us confidence in ourselves to talk and argue intelligently."

"Five points of view give a better concept than one."

"I have to hold my own in the group so must have more than one answer to many of the questions."

"The group is more informal and we really talk because we're left to ourselves."

                    "AGAINST"

"Some accepted what was said uncritically."

"I get better results studying alone."

"So many personal opinions were expressed that we were often unable to find out an answer to a question which we agreed to."

"Procedure technique should have been definitely taught at the beginning of the term."

"I did not like the period because my group covered too little ground and spent too much time arguing."

"In our group some girls did the work and those who weren't sincere had a chance to shirk."

"Our group deteriorated into a library period or reading period."

APPENDIX C

SAMPLE TEST QUESTIONS

YES AND NO

INTRA-TERM EXAMINATIONS
(INSTRUCTOR'S)

FINAL EXAMINATION
(DEPARTMENT'S)

____ 1. Must there be an integration of formal and informal educational activities if the most effective results are to be achieved?

____ 1. Does formal education do away with the need for informal education?

____ 2. Since principles are statements of general truths should they be subject to change if society is to have any stability?

____ 2. Can a principle considered immutable care for life in a changing civilization?

____ 3. Must the child of to-day attend school if he is to have the ability to adjust effectively to life situations?

____ 3. Will education insure increased competency on the part of the one receiving it?

____ 4. Is reasoning independent of instinctive reactions and organized habits?

____ 4. In a problem does the mere presence of difficulty motivate and sustain thinking?

____ 5. Does knowledge of what is considered right and wrong insure wise moral choices?

____ 5. Does moral conduct depend to a great degree upon intelligence?

____ 6. Is a sound philosophy of education quite essential to good practice as a science of education?

____ 6. Does philosophy aid man in solving problems for which there is no scientific solution?

____ 7. Has the traditional school taught information in its functional relation to activity?

____ 7. Does modern education place less value upon knowledge and information than did the school of yesterday?

____ 8. Does man have to change both his environment and himself before effective life adjustments are possible?

____ 8. Would the knowledge that a cure for cancer had been discovered insure its benefit to humanity?

____ 9. Does Dewey's philosophy disregard preparation for adult life?

____ 9. Is Dewey's philosophy pragmatic?

____10. Is the mother in her kitchen teaching her daughter how to bake a cake an illustration of formal education?

____10. Must an individual go to an educational institution in order to get formal education?

MULTIPLE CHOICE (BEST ANSWER)

INTRA-TERM TEST

1. Informal education:
   a) always existed
   b) began with the family
   c) began with the tribe

2. The formulation of definite aims of education should:
   a) be encouraged because they offer tentative goals
   b) not be encouraged because they may lead to hypocrisy
   c) be encouraged because they are infallible guides

3. Knowledge is valuable because it is:
   a) concerned with truth
   b) an essential means of promoting human welfare
   c) concerned with accumulation of facts

4. Children will probably acquire the best understanding of civic efficiency by:
   a) learning abstract civic principles
   b) understanding the function of legislative and judicial offices
   c) participating in democratic school life

5. To secure a transfer of desirable attitudes from family situations to larger social situations we must provide:
   a) accurate knowledge about people
   b) suitable contacts with people

FINAL EXAMINATION

1. The value of a school subject may best be judged by:
   a) the facts it sets forth
   b) its usefulness in developing resources for adjustment
   c) its interest for the pupil

2. Constructive activities are valuable because:
   a) they are fitted to express abstract ideas
   b) they economize time
   c) they increase motive power through interest in the concrete

3. Advantageous changes in the world's things produce their benefits only when accompanied by:
   a) changes in traditions
   b) changes in inventions
   c) changes in human nature

4. A grave danger of formal education as it is still conceived to-day is that there is:
   a) little opportunity for development of creative ability
   b) no provision for individual differences
   c) very little emphasis on knowledge

5. Education is chiefly concerned with:
   a) methods of teaching various subjects
   b) interactions of human individuals and their world

ASSOCIATION QUESTIONS

Before each number place the letter of the phrase which suggests the best psychological association.

INTRA-TERM TEST

1. Insanity	*a.* A recessive trait
2. Chromosomes	*b.* Dominant and recessive traits
3. Evolution	*c.* Carriers of determining hereditary bodies
4. Mendel	*d.* Continuity only through germ plasm
5. Lamarcke	*e.* Inheritance of acquired characteristics
6. Heredity	*f.* Intermarriage of strong strains
7. Darwin	*g.* Development through change over a long
8. Weisman	period of time
9. Eugenics	*h.* Natural selection
10. Galton	*i.* Antecedents of geniuses
	j. Sum total of resemblances between parents and offspring

FINAL EXAMINATION

1. Adolescence	*a.* Emotional unrest
2. Elementary school	*b.* Degree of craving for a particular activity
3. Theory of compensation	
4. Human inability to adjust at birth	*c.* Motor helplessness
5. Pre-school	*d.* Strength in one trait accompanied by strength in another trait
6. High school	*e.* Body of knowledge common to all
7. University	*f.* Transition schooling
8. Junior high school	*g.* Direct experience with immediate environment
9. Theory of correlation	*h.* Differential education
10. Readiness	*i.* High degree of specialization
	j. Weakness in one trait accompanied by strength in another

COMPLETION QUESTIONS

Fill each blank with a word or words which best complete the meaning of the statement.

INTRA-TERM TEST

1. The theory of correlation assumes that strength in one trait is accompanied by _____ in another trait.
2. High school attendance has increased about ____% between 1890 and 1925.
3. _____ experimentally proved adult education to be feasible.
4. _____ wrote "The Child-Centered School."
5. The A. Q. is found by dividing the _____ by the _____.

FINAL EXAMINATION

1. The theory of compensation assumes that strength in one trait is accompanied by _____ in another trait.
2. College attendance has increased about ____% between 1890 and 1925.
3. _____ first made intelligence testing practical for classroom use.
4. _____ wrote "Democracy and Education."
5. The I. Q. is found by dividing the _____ by the _____.

APPENDIX D

NORMAL FREQUENCY DISTRIBUTION *

Base-Line Laid off in ½ P.E.'s

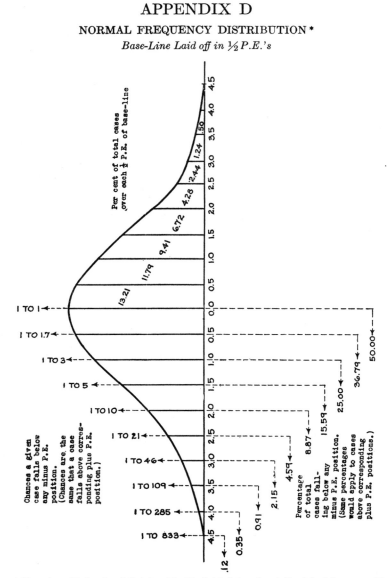

* Chart from McGaughy, J. Ralph. *The Fiscal Administration of City School Systems*, p. 71.
The Macmillan Co., New York, 1924.

52